Autism & PDD
Primary Social Skills

Behavior

by Pam Britton Reese and Nena C. Challenner

Skills	Ages	Grades
■ social skills ■ language	■ 3 through 8	■ PreK through 3

Evidence-Based Practice

- Children with autism need approaches that focus on social functioning. These approaches should be introduced as ongoing intervention strategies from early years to adulthood (RCSLT, 2005).

- Many children with autism spectrum disorders (ASD) learn more readily through the visual modality (RCSLT, 2005).

- Visual supports enhance language comprehension for individuals on the autism spectrum, bridging communication between the individuals and the social expectations of the world around them (Hodgdon, 1995).

- Stories about specific social situations help students with ASD understand and respond to similar social situations appropriately (Kuoch & Mirenda, 2003).

Autism & PDD Primary Social Skills Lessons incorporates these principles and is also based on expert professional practice.

References
Hodgdon, L. (1995). *Visual strategies for improving communication.* Troy, MI: QuirkRoberts Publishing.

Kuoch, H., & Mirenda, P. (2003). Social story interventions for young children with autism spectrum disorders. *Focus on Autism and Other Developmental Disabilities, 18,* 219-227.

Royal College of Speech & Language Therapists (RCSLT). (2005). *Clinical guidelines for speech & language therapists.* Retrieved June 29, 2009, from www.rcslt.org/resources/clinicalguidelines

LinguiSystems

LinguiSystems, Inc.
3100 4th Avenue
East Moline, IL 61244
800-776-4332

FAX: 800-577-4555
Email: service@linguisystems.com
Web: linguisystems.com

Copyright © 1999 LinguiSystems, Inc.

All of our products are copyrighted to protect the fine work of our authors. You may only copy the student lessons and tracking forms as needed for your own use. Any other reproduction or distribution of the pages in this book is prohibited, including copying the entire book to use as another primary source or "master" copy.

Printed in the U.S.A.

ISBN 10: 0-7606-0299-9
ISBN 13: 978-0-7606-0299-7

About the Authors

Pam Britton Reese, M.A., CCC-SLP, owns a private practice, CommunicAid Plus, where she provides speech and language services to children and adults. She is also an educational consultant to public and private schools. Pam has over 9 years experience in the schools as a speech-language pathologist and teacher of the hearing-impaired. She has worked with young children with autism and PDD since 1995. *Autism & PDD: Social Skills Lessons* is her first publication with LinguiSystems.

Nena C. Challenner, B.S., is a PPCD (Preschool Program for Children with Disabilities) Instructor and Inclusion Specialist. She has been a teacher for over 15 years and has taught preschool through second grade. She has worked with children with autism and PDD since 1995. *Autism & PDD: Social Skills Lessons* is her first publication with LinguiSystems.

Acknowledgments

Thanks to my husband, Joe, for his support and enthusiasm, and to my children, Kate, Matthew, and Sam for their patience and understanding – PBR

Thanks to my parents, Glen A. Zachary and Betty Y. Zachary, for their love and encouragement that will be with me always, and to my husband, Phillip, and my son, Ryan, for their patience and support throughout the writing of this book – NCC

And thanks to Amy Ballard for sharing her artistic ability on our very first social lesson, to Julie Nelson for sharing her wide expertise on children's behavior, and to Judy Walling, Special Education Director, Midlothian ISD, for expanding the world of children with special needs.

Dedication

To Shawn, for showing us a way to teach children with autism

Illustrations by Eulala Conner
Page Layout by Christine Buysse

Table of Contents

Copyright © 1999 LinguiSystems, Inc.

Introduction

A few years ago, we were working together to facilitate the inclusion of a five-year-old boy with autism into a kindergarten/first-grade classroom. Communication with the child was a problem. Although the classroom had been structured to aid his inclusion, inappropriate behaviors repeatedly set him back both academically and socially. Some of his typical behaviors were climbing on desktops, darting, squirting glue on tables, dumping toys, and pulling on electrical cords.

We learned of Carol Gray's success with stories describing social situations to teach children with autism. The format of Gray's stories in *The New Social Story Book* (1994) seemed perfect for our student. However, due to the child's young age, we soon found that those stories were too long. Shorter sentences and stories plus the addition of pictures were critical to his comprehension. So we began writing one-page lessons with each sentence supported by one or more pictures. Our lessons targeted typical needs of preschool and early primary students.

Our lessons were so successful that we began using them with other children with autism and PDD. As parents began to see how the lessons worked at school, they requested lessons concerning behaviors at home and in the community. In addition, the lessons were used successfully with children with other disabilities and with typically-developing children. *Autism & PDD: Social Skills Lessons* is the culmination of the work we did with teachers and families over the last few years.

About the Books

The lessons are grouped into five separate books:

- School
- Home
- Community
- Getting Along
- Behavior

In each book, we have included two types of lessons: instructional and behavioral. The instructional lessons are intended to teach young children what they need to do or say in social situations that are often overwhelming to children with autism (e.g., *Receiving a Compliment*, Getting Along book, page 13). The instructional lessons can be used as part of a social skills curriculum with small groups of children or individuals. The behavioral lessons target specific social problems that need to be stopped. They are best used with an individual child (e.g., *Running Away (Darting)*, Behavior book, page 27).

The lessons are not intended to be used in the order presented, but chosen according to the needs of a particular child.

Behavior lessons are not for everyone. The lessons in this book should only be used if the problem exists. Children with autism will sometimes act out aggressively toward self and others when frustrated or angry because they are unable to communicate how they feel. Immediate intervention by a teacher, parent, or caregiver is necessary when safety is the issue. The lessons in this book should be used after the child has calmed down, NOT while a dangerous behavior is occurring.

                    Copyright © 1999 LinguiSystems, Inc.

Make the Lessons Fit the Child

No two children are the same! Although the lessons are ready for use as they appear in the books, it will undoubtedly be necessary to make changes in some lessons to fit the child. For example, some children may not understand that the generic child used in the lessons refers to them. For these children, attach a photograph of the child in the upper right-hand corner of the lesson. As you read the story, point to the photograph and say the child's name in place of any pronouns. Continue to use the lesson as written. In time, some children may learn to accept the use of the generic child.

Editing may also be needed if the chosen lesson does not exactly match what the child is doing. For example, in the *Squirting Glue* lesson (Behavior book, page 15), we show the child squirting glue on tables. If the child is squirting glue on the floor or on other children, you will need to change the lesson. Cross out the text and rewrite the sentence following the format of the original sentence.

Blank lines have been inserted in the text in some lessons to help you individualize them for each child. There are empty spaces above the lines for additional pictures if needed. The picture index in the back of each book contains pictures that may be copied and substituted. If you can't find the picture you need in the index, feel free to substitute or add photographs, your own line drawings, copies of pictures from another lesson in one of the other books, *Boardmaker* Software (1995), or other computer-generated clip art.

Using the Lessons

Identify the skill to be taught. No child will need every lesson. Search for the source of the problem. Is it sensory? Is it a communication breakdown? Is the child sick? Some problems can be solved by ignoring the behavior or changing something in the environment. Limit the number of lessons presented at one time. Start with one or two. Wait until they are learned before introducing more.

Choose the appropriate lesson and make two copies. Change the story as needed. Place one copy of the lesson in a notebook for the child. As skills are presented and learned, the notebook can be used for reviewing lessons with the child and for sharing the lessons with other teachers, parents, and caregivers. The second copy is to be used for direct instruction with the child as follows:

1. Identify the time and place the social situation occurs. The *Tracking Multiple Behaviors* form, page 50, and/or the *Initial Behavior Analysis* form, page 52, will help you.

2. When teaching a new skill, the social lesson should immediately precede the targeted situation. For example, if the child is having a problem completing seatwork, read *I Finish My Work* (School book, page 14) just before you hand out the work.

3. Present the lesson. Sit with the child one-on-one in a quiet area and read the lesson aloud. Point to the pictures for emphasis. Read the lesson again.

4. Allow the child to keep the lesson. This allows the child to review the lesson repeatedly as the new skill is learned. Don't worry if this copy is damaged or discarded by the child since you have another copy in the child's notebook.

6

Copyright © 1999 LinguiSystems, Inc.

5. Document the lesson(s) taught using the *Record of Progress*, page 54, and/or the tracking forms on pages 56-59. These records can serve as documentation for IEP objectives and behavioral intervention.

Special Considerations

Pronouns can be difficult for some children with autism. We have used "I" extensively throughout the books as a way to help teach the pronoun. If pronoun use prevents comprehension of the lesson, substitute the child's name in the text and/or use the child's photograph in place of the "I" symbol.

Be sure to use words that the child is familiar with (e.g., gym vs. P.E.; jungle gym vs. monkey bars).

The lesson and pictures on one page may be overwhelming for some children. You can use a blank sheet of paper to mask the rest of the lesson as you read each line. The lessons can also be used to make a small book. Cut apart the sentences and accompanying pictures. Place each sentence/pictures in the center of a separate sheet of paper. Staple the pages together to make a book.

These lessons can easily be adapted to the child's language and comprehension level. If necessary, delete words to shorten sentences. Some children may also need fewer pictures per sentence. We have even used lessons with no text for behavior (e.g., bite/time-out) and instruction (e.g., work/computer).

Adult: "If I bite (point), time out (point)."

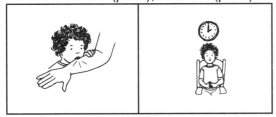

Adult: "If I finish work (point), computer (point)."

These lessons do not offer a solution to the myriad of challenges presented by young children with autism and PDD. They have, however, proved to be a useful tool for many families, teachers, and speech-language pathologists to teach children with autism and PDD to understand the social world in which they live. We hope that you will find these social skills lessons as effective as we have.

Pam and Nena

7

Copyright © 1999 LinguiSystems, Inc.

Behavior Note

I had bad behavior at school.

My teacher will write a note to _____.
(person)

My teacher will put the note in my backpack.

I will leave the note in my backpack.

I will show the note to _____.
(person)

My Parent Talks to My Teacher

_____ talks to my teacher.
(person)

I do not pull on _____.
(person)

I look at a book.

I wait quietly.

_____ is happy.
(person)

Tearing

I draw on paper.

I write on paper.

I do not tear my paper.

I do not tear a friend's paper.

I write or draw on paper.

My teacher is happy.

Copyright © 1999 LinguiSystems, Inc.

Climbing on Furniture

I go to my desk.

I sit in my chair.

I do not climb on desks.

I may fall.

I sit in my chair.

My teacher is happy.

Copyright © 1999 LinguiSystems, Inc.

Toys Stay at School

There are toys at school.

Toys stay at school.

I do not take school toys home.

I play with school toys at school.

My teacher is happy.

Copyright © 1999 LinguiSystems, Inc.

Falling on Friends

I sit with friends on the floor.

I cross my legs.

I keep my hands in my lap.

I do not fall back on friends.

I sit on my bottom.

My teacher is happy.

Squirting Glue

Glue is for work. Glue goes on paper.

I do not grab glue.

I do not squeeze glue on tables.

I squeeze glue gently on paper.

My teacher is happy.

Dumping Toys

Toys are in tubs.

I take out a handful.

I do not dump toys.

I only play with one tub.

Time to stop playing. I clean up.

Counting

I like to count.

I count by myself.

Sometimes friends do not want to count.

Sometimes my teacher does not want to count.

I count by myself. It is okay.

Backpack

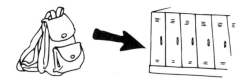

I put my backpack in my locker.

I do not wear it at recess.

I do not wear it at lunch.

Time to go home.*

I get my backpack.

* Add hands to clock to show time school dismisses.

I Like My Things

I like _____.
(favorite items)

I can have them at home.

I can take _____ with me in the car.
(number)

1

I can take one in the store.

_____ will help me choose.
(person)

I can have all of my things at home.

Mouth Noises

Sometimes I make a noise with my mouth.

It sounds like _____.
(noise*)

People don't like that noise.

I keep my mouth quiet.

People are happy.

*Substitute any sound specific to the child.

Copyright © 1999 LinguiSystems, Inc.

Cursing

I do not say bad words.

People do not like bad words.

Sometimes I hear bad words. I will try not to say them.

_____ says, "No bad words."

I will try not to say bad words.

Stealing Money

_____ gives me money.
(person)

I use my money at school.

I see friends' money.   It is not my money.

I do not touch friends' money.

_____ gives me money.
(person)

Drawing on the Wall

I draw on paper.

I use crayons or pencils or markers to draw on paper.

I do not draw on the wall with crayons.

I do not draw on the wall with pencils.

I do not draw on the wall with markers.

I draw on paper.

VCR/DVD Player Buttons

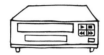

The VCR/DVD player has buttons.

I do not touch the buttons on the VCR/DVD player.

I sit down. I wait.

_____ pushes the buttons.
(person)

I watch a movie.

I will try not to touch the buttons on the VCR/DVD player.

Copyright © 1999 LinguiSystems, Inc.

VCR Tapes

 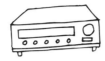

Only tapes go in the VCR.

 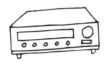

I do not put toys in the VCR.

 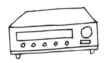

I do not put food in the VCR.

 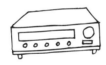

I do not put crayons in the VCR.

 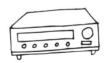

Only tapes go in the VCR.

Electrical Cords

The computer has a cord. The lamp has a cord.

I do not touch cords. This is important.

Cords are hot.

_____ moves cords.
(person)

My teacher moves cords.

I do not touch cords.

Running Away (Darting)

I walk by _____.
                (person)

I do not run from _____.
                        (person)

I hold _____'s hand.
            (person)

_____ says, "Stop."   I stand still.
      (person)

I walk beside _____.
                    (person)

_____ is happy when I walk nearby.
      (person)

Shoelaces

People need shoelaces in their shoes.

Shoelaces keep shoes on feet.

Sometimes I take shoelaces out of shoes.

I will try to put shoelaces back in shoes.

_____ is happy when shoes have shoelaces.
(person)

Sharing Furniture

I like to sit on the _____ chair.
                        (color)

_____ can sit on the _____ chair.
   (person)   (color)

I like to sit on the couch.

_____ can sit on the couch.
   (person)

I will let _____ sit on the chair or couch.
               (person)

People are happy when I share.

What Goes in the Toilet?

_____ goes in the toilet.
(tee-tee/poop*)

Some toilet paper goes in the toilet.

I do not put my hands in the toilet.

I do not put _____ in the toilet.
(thing)

Only _____ and some toilet paper go in the toilet.
(tee-tee/poop*)

*Substitute any word the child is familiar with.

Flushing the Toilet

When I finish using the toilet, I flush it.

I only flush one time.

It sounds like "swish" and "gurgle."

It is okay. The noise will stop.

I only flush one time.

Grabbing Someone's Chin

I want _____ to look at me.
(person)

I say, "Look, _____."
(person)

I do not grab _____'s chin.
(person)

_____ does not like it.
(person)

I wait. _____ will look at me.
(person)

_____ is happy when I wait.
(person)

Copyright © 1999 LinguiSystems, Inc.

Pinching

Sometimes I feel mad.*

I do not pinch people.

Pinching hurts.

 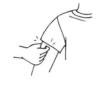

_____ does not like pinching.
(person)

I do not pinch friends.

I say, "I am mad.*"

*Substitute appropriate feeling (e.g.,
playful, scared, happy, confused).

Copyright © 1999 LinguiSystems, Inc.

Hitting

Sometimes I feel mad.*

I do not hit people.

Hitting hurts.

_____ does not like hitting.
(person)

I do not hit friends.

I say, "I am mad.*"

*Substitute appropriate feeling (e.g.,
playful, scared, happy, confused).

Biting

Sometimes I feel mad.*

I do not bite people.

Biting hurts.

_____ does not like biting.
(person)

I do not bite friends.

I say, "I am mad.*"

*Substitute appropriate feeling (e.g., playful, scared, happy, confused).

Scratching

Sometimes I feel mad.*

I do not scratch people.

Scratching hurts.

_____ does not like scratching.
 (person)

I do not scratch friends.

I say, "I am mad.*"

*Substitute appropriate feeling (e.g., playful, scared, happy, confused).

Copyright © 1999 LinguiSystems, Inc.

Kicking

Sometimes I feel mad.*

I do not kick people.

Kicking hurts.

_____ does not like kicking.
(person)

I do not kick friends.

I say, "I am mad.*"

*Substitute appropriate feeling (e.g., playful, scared, happy, confused).

Copyright © 1999 LinguiSystems, Inc.

Pulling Hair

Sometimes I feel mad.*

I do not pull hair.

Pulling hair hurts.

_____ does not like pulling hair.
(person)

I do not pull friends' hair.

I say, "I am mad.*"

*Substitute appropriate feeling (e.g., playful, scared, happy, confused).

Copyright © 1999 LinguiSystems, Inc.

Choking

Sometimes I feel mad.*

I do not choke people.

Choking hurts.

_____ does not like choking.
(person)

I do not choke friends.

I say, "I am mad.*"

*Substitute appropriate feeling (e.g., playful, scared, happy, confused).

Pushing

Sometimes I feel mad.*

I do not push people.

Pushing hurts.

_____ does not like pushing.
(person)

I do not push friends.

I say, "I am mad.*"

*Substitute appropriate feeling (e.g.,
playful, scared, happy, confused).

Copyright © 1999 LinguiSystems, Inc.

Throwing

Sometimes I feel mad.*

I do not throw things at people.

Throwing things hurts.

_____ does not like throwing.
(person)

I do not throw things at friends.

I say, "I am mad.*"

*Substitute appropriate feeling (e.g., playful, scared, happy, confused).

Copyright © 1999 LinguiSystems, Inc.

Head Butting

Sometimes I feel mad.*

I do not hit _____ with my head.

(person)

I do not hit friends with my head.

Hitting with my head hurts.

_____ does not like me to hit people with my head.

(person)

I say, "I am mad.*"

*Substitute appropriate feeling (e.g., playful, scared, happy, confused).

Copyright © 1999 LinguiSystems, Inc.

Spitting

I do not spit my saliva.

does not like spitting.

Saliva stays in my mouth.

I swallow my saliva.

I do not spit my saliva.

Breaking Toys

Sometimes I am mad.*

I do not break toys.

_____ does not like it when I break toys.
(person)

I say, "I am mad.*"

I do not break toys.

*Substitute appropriate feeling (e.g., playful, scared, happy, confused).

Copyright © 1999 LinguiSystems, Inc.

Biting Myself

I feel mad.*

I feel scared.

I will try not to bite myself.

Biting hurts.

I squeeze my hands together.

I will try not to bite myself.

*Substitute appropriate feeling (e.g., playful, scared, happy, confused).

Pulling Out Own Hair

I get mad.*

I do not pull my hair out.

Pulling hair hurts.

I squeeze my hands together.

I say, "I am mad.*"

I do not pull my hair out.

*Substitute appropriate feeling (e.g., playful, scared, happy, confused).

Overeating

I eat my food.

I ask for more. I only get a little.

Now I am finished.

I do not eat more food.

I do not ask for more.

Eating too much makes me sick.

Hurting Animals

I am gentle with my _____.
(animal)

I do not twist my _____'s ears.
(animal)

I do not pull my _____'s tail.
(animal)

I do not grab the _____.
(animal)

I pet my _____ softly.
(animal)

I am gentle with my _____.
(animal)

Copyright © 1999 LinguiSystems, Inc.

Picture Index

People

Places

music class   gym/P.E.   art class

Animals

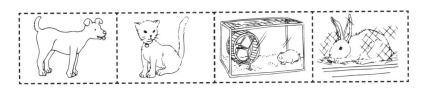

Tracking Multiple Behaviors

Child's Name _____   Date _____

Behavior		Behavior		Behavior		Behavior		Behavior	
Time 1	Location	Time 1	Location	Time 1	Location	Time 1	Location	Time 1	Location
Antecedent		Antecedent		Antecedent		Antecedent		Antecedent	
Consequence		Consequence		Consequence		Consequence		Consequence	
Time 2	Location	Time 2	Location	Time 2	Location	Time 2	Location	Time 2	Location
Antecedent		Antecedent		Antecedent		Antecedent		Antecedent	
Consequence		Consequence		Consequence		Consequence		Consequence	
Time 3	Location	Time 3	Location	Time 3	Location	Time 3	Location	Time 3	Location
Antecedent		Antecedent		Antecedent		Antecedent		Antecedent	
Consequence		Consequence		Consequence		Consequence		Consequence	
Time 4	Location	Time 4	Location	Time 4	Location	Time 4	Location	Time 4	Location
Antecedent		Antecedent		Antecedent		Antecedent		Antecedent	
Consequence		Consequence		Consequence		Consequence		Consequence	

Copyright © 1999 LinguiSystems, Inc.

Tracking Multiple Behaviors Example

Child's Name *Danny W.*   Date _____

Behavior *Biting Self*		Behavior *Biting Others*		Behavior *Scratching Others*		Behavior *Hitting Others*		Behavior	
Time 1 9:35	Location circle time	Time 1 10:05	Location block center	Time 1 10:50	Location in line	Time 1 11:15	Location snack table	Time 1	Location
Antecedent ?		Antecedent wanted adult to sit by him		Antecedent another student was talking to him		Antecedent another student bumped his arm		Antecedent	
Consequence 5 min. time-out		Consequence redirected		Consequence time-out		Consequence apology/moved to another chair		Consequence	
Time 2	Location	Time 2 10:15	Location house center	Time 2	Location	Time 2	Location	Time 2	Location
Antecedent		Antecedent friend had doll he wanted		Antecedent		Antecedent		Antecedent	
Consequence		Consequence redirected		Consequence		Consequence		Consequence	
Time 3	Location	Time 3	Location	Time 3	Location	Time 3	Location	Time 3	Location
Antecedent		Antecedent		Antecedent		Antecedent		Antecedent	
Consequence		Consequence		Consequence		Consequence		Consequence	
Time 4	Location	Time 4	Location	Time 4	Location	Time 4	Location	Time 4	Location
Antecedent		Antecedent		Antecedent		Antecedent		Antecedent	
Consequence		Consequence		Consequence		Consequence		Consequence	

                                    Copyright © 1999 LinguiSystems, Inc.

Initial Behavior Analysis*

Child's Name _____   Date _____

Setting _____   Activity _____

Name of Person Completing Form _____

What happened just before the behavior occurred? _____

_____

_____

Describe the behavior. _____

_____

_____

What was the consequence of the behavior? _____

_____

_____

Date/Time	Location	No. of Occurrences	Consequences

Comments: _____

---

* This form can be used for observing the same behavior several times in one day or for observation over several days.

Copyright © 1999 LinguiSystems, Inc.

Initial Behavior Analysis Example*

Child's Name ___*Cindy B.*___   Date ___*3/15 – 3/19*___

Setting ___*kindergarten classroom*___   Activity ___*story time*___

Name of Person Completing Form _____

What happened just before the behavior occurred? ___*children sat on floor to hear*___

___*teacher read story*_____

_____

Describe the behavior. ___*repeatedly fell backward onto other children*___

_____

_____

What was the consequence of the behavior? ___*removed to sit in chair at desk during*___

___*story after several requests to stop*_____

_____

Date/Time	Location	No. of Occurrences	Consequences
3/15	*book center*	*I I I*	*redirected 2x, moved to chair*
3/16	*book center*	*I I I I*	*redirected 3x, moved to chair*
3/17	*book center*	*I I I*	*redirected 2x, moved to chair*
3/18	*book center*	*I I I*	*redirected 2x, moved to chair***
3/19	*book center*	*I I*	*redirected 1x, moved to chair*

Comments: ___*** 3/18 – After being put in chair, she screamed and was removed to hallway.*___

_____

* This form can be used for observing the same behavior several times in one day or for observation over several days.

Record of Progress

Child's Name _____

Behavior _____

Social Skill Lesson _____

Date Social Skill Lesson Initiated _____

Intervention Chart

Baseline _____ (average # of occurrences in one day from *Initial Behavior Analysis*)

	Lesson Read?		How often does the behavior occur?								
	Yes	No									
Day 1											
Day 2											
Day 3											
Day 4											
Day 5											
Day 6											
Day 7											
Day 8											
Day 9											
Day 10											

Comments: _____

_____

_____

_____

Record of Progress Example

Child's Name ___*Cindy B.*___

Behavior ___*falling back on other children during story time*___

Social Skill Lesson ___*Falling on Friends (Behavior)*___

Date Social Skill Lesson Initiated ___*3/18*___

Intervention Chart

Baseline ___*3x/day*___ (average # of occurrences in one day from *Initial Behavior Analysis*)

	Lesson Read?		How often does the behavior occur?										
	Yes	No											
Day 1	X		*0*										
Day 2	X		*0*										
Day 3		X	✓	✓	✓								
Day 4	X		*0*										
Day 5	X		*0*										
Day 6	X		*0*										
Day 7		X	*0*										
Day 8													
Day 9													
Day 10													

Comments: _____

_____

_____

_____

55

Copyright © 1999 LinguiSystems, Inc.

Tracking Form for Lessons – Individual

Child's Name _____

School Behavior

☐ Behavior Note
Date _____

_____

☐ My Parent Talks to My Teacher
Date _____

_____

☐ Tearing
Date _____

_____

☐ Climbing on Furniture
Date _____

_____

☐ Toys Stay at School
Date _____

_____

☐ Falling on Friends
Date _____

_____

☐ Squirting Glue
Date _____

_____

☐ Dumping Toys
Date _____

_____

☐ Counting
Date _____

_____

☐ Backpack
Date _____

_____

☐ I Like My Things
Date _____

_____

☐ Mouth Noises
Date _____

_____

☐ Cursing
Date _____

_____

☐ Stealing Money
Date _____

_____

Home Behavior

☐ Drawing on the Wall
Date _____

_____

☐ VCR/DVD Player Buttons
Date _____

_____

☐ VCR Tapes
Date _____

_____

☐ Electrical Cords
Date _____

_____

☐ Running Away (Darting)
Date _____

_____

☐ Shoelaces
Date _____

_____

Child's Name _____

Home Behavior, *continued*

❑ Sharing Furniture
Date _____
_____
_____

❑ What Goes in the Toilet?
Date _____
_____
_____

❑ Flushing the Toilet
Date _____
_____
_____

Hurting Self/Others

❑ Grabbing Someone's Chin
Date _____
_____
_____

❑ Pinching
Date _____
_____
_____

❑ Hitting
Date _____
_____
_____

❑ Biting
Date _____
_____
_____

❑ Scratching
Date _____
_____
_____

❑ Kicking
Date _____
_____
_____

❑ Pulling Hair
Date _____
_____
_____

❑ Choking
Date _____
_____
_____

❑ Pushing
Date _____
_____
_____

❑ Throwing
Date _____
_____
_____

❑ Head Butting
Date _____
_____
_____

❑ Spitting
Date _____
_____
_____

❑ Breaking Toys
Date _____
_____
_____

❑ Biting Myself
Date _____
_____
_____

❑ Pulling Out Own Hair
Date _____
_____
_____

❑ Overeating
Date _____
_____
_____

❑ Hurting Animals
Date _____
_____
_____

Tracking Form for Lessons – Group						Behavior
Names:						
School Behavior						
Behavior Note						
My Parent Talks to My Teacher						
Tearing						
Climbing on Furniture						
Toys Stay at School						
Falling on Friends						
Squirting Glue						
Dumping Toys						
Counting						
Backpack						
I Like My Things						
Mouth Noises						
Cursing						
Stealing Money						
Home Behavior						
Drawing on the Wall						
VCR/DVD Player Buttons						
VCR Tapes						
Electrical Cords						
Running Away (Darting)						
Shoelaces						
Sharing Furniture						
What Goes in the Toilet?						
Flushing the Toilet						
Hurting Self/Others						
Grabbing Someone's Chin						
Pinching						
Hitting						
Biting						
Scratching						
Kicking						

 Copyright © 1999 LinguiSystems, Inc.

Tracking Form for Lessons – Group, *continued*	Behavior					
Names:						
Hurting Self/Others, *cont.*						
Pulling Hair						
Choking						
Pushing						
Throwing						
Head Butting						
Spitting						
Breaking Toys						
Biting Myself						
Pulling Out Own Hair						
Overeating						
Hurting Animals						

Copyright © 1999 LinguiSystems, Inc.

Overview of Lessons

Getting Along

Social Interactions
Saying "Hi" I
When I Talk to People I
Introducing Myself I
Mr. and Mrs. I
Receiving a Compliment I
Let Others Talk . . . . B
Saying Good-bye at School . . . B
Getting Attention . . . . B
Hearing "No" . . . . B
Saying "I'm Sorry" . . . . I/B
Requesting I
Saying "Please" and
 "Thank You" I
Complying with a Request . . . I/B
Asking to Use the Bathroom . . . I
Shutting the Bathroom Door . . . I
Sharing . . . . I/B
Showing Affection I
Holding a Door I
Answering the Phone I
Answering the Door I
Getting Picture Taken I
Interacting with a Baby I
Playing a Board Game I
Keeping My Shirt Down . . . . B
Keeping My Clothes On . . . . B
Other People's Glasses . . . . B
Other People's Watches . . . . B
Saying Nice Things I

Eating
Asking for More Food . . . . . I/B
Eating Slowly . . . . B
Using a Napkin I
Chewing Food I
Taking Only One . . . . I/B
Drinking from My Glass . . . I/B
Chewing Gum . . . . I/B
Eating Off the Floor . . . . B

My Body
Using a Tissue I
Fingers in My Nose . . . . B
Fingers in My Mouth . . . . B
Sticking Out My Tongue . . . . B

Behavior*

School Behavior
Behavior Note
My Parent Talks to My Teacher
Tearing
Climbing on Furniture
Toys Stay at School
Falling on Friends
Squirting Glue
Dumping Toys
Counting
Backpack
I Like My Things
Mouth Noises
Cursing
Stealing Money

Home Behavior
Drawing on the Wall
VCR/DVD Player Buttons
VCR Tapes
Electrical Cords
Running Away (Darting)
Shoelaces
Sharing Furniture
What Goes in the Toilet?
Flushing the Toilet

Hurting Self/Others
Grabbing Someone's Chin
Pinching
Hitting
Biting
Scratching
Kicking
Pulling Hair
Choking
Pushing
Throwing
Head Butting
Spitting
Breaking Toys
Biting Myself
Pulling Out Own Hair
Overeating
Hurting Animals

Home

Daily Routines
Morning Routine I
Getting Dressed I
Wearing Different Clothes . . . B
Mealtime: I Eat My
 Own Food . . . . B
Trying New Food . . . . I/B
Going to Bed . . . . I/B
Weekend Morning . . . . I/B
Cleaning My Room . . . . I/B
After-school Day-care . . . . . I/B

Self-Care
Brushing Teeth I
Shampooing Hair I
Clipping Fingernails I
Bath Time I
Using the Toilet I
Taking Medicine I

Appliances/Safety
Answering Machine . . . . B
The Vacuum Cleaner . . . . . . B
Electrical Outlets . . . . B
Hot and Cold Water I
Hot Iron I
Hot Stove I
The Microwave . . . . B
Wearing My Seat Belt . . . . . . B
Sitting in the Back Seat . . . . . B

Family Relations
Getting Help . . . . I/B
Others Talking on the Phone . . B
Favorite TV Show . . . . B
Watching One TV . . . . B
Sharing the TV . . . . B
Sharing the Computer . . . . . . B
Pets I
People Go Away I
The Baby-sitter I

Special Occasions
Not Going on a Trip I
Staying Away from Home I
Time-out . . . . B
Sick Sibling Stays Home I
Having Company . . . . B
My Birthday I
The Sprinkler I

I = Instructional
B = Behavioral

* All lessons are behavioral.

Overview of Lessons, *continued*

School

Routine Activities
First Day of School I
Riding the Bus to School I
Saying the Pledge of Allegiance I
Using a Schedule I
Using a Work Table I
I Finish My Work I
Listening to My Teacher Read a Story I
Listening to Friends Read Books I
Recess I
Cafeteria: Choosing Food . . . . I/B
Cafeteria: Carrying My Tray I
Cafeteria: I Eat My Own Food . . . . B
Cafeteria: Waiting with Friends . . . . B
Nap Time I
Using Math Manipulatives . . . . I/B
Using Markers . . . . I/B
Using the Computer . . . . I/B
Cleaning Up the Room . . . . I/B

Extra-Curricular Activities
Transitions I
Gym Class I
Going to Speech I
Library I

Social Skills
Quiet Voice . . . . I/B
Raising My Hand . . . . I/B
Waiting for Help . . . . I/B
Walking in Line . . . . I/B

Special Days
Going to an Event I
Field Trip I
Somebody Different Picks Me Up I
Holidays Away from School I
My Teacher Is Sick I
Fire Drill I
Tornado Drill I

Self-Care
Dirty Hands I
Washing Hands I
Using the Rest Room I
Covering My Cough and Sneeze I
Wearing a Helmet I
Going to the School Nurse I
Getting My Temperature Taken I

I = Instructional
B = Behavioral

Community*

Community Services
The Haircut
The Dentist
A Cavity
The Check-up
Immunizations
Shopping
The Car Wash
The Post Office
New Shoes
New Clothes
The Library: Choosing Books
The Library: Story Time
The Video Store
The Restaurant
Fast Food
Drive-Thru Food

Social Activities
Visiting a Friend's House
The Birthday Party
The Movie Theater
The Skating Rink
The Swimming Pool
The Zoo
The Park
The Picnic
Taking a Vacation
Camping
Fishing
Soccer Practice
The Soccer Game
The T-Ball Game
The Parade
The Clown
Fireworks

Transportation
The Airplane
The Boat Ride
The Bus Ride
The Elevator
The Escalator

Safety
Crossing the Street
I Can't Find My Parent

* All lessons are instructional.

References and Resources

Frith, U. *Autism: Explaining the Enigma*. Oxford, England: Blackwell, 1989.

Grandin, T. *Thinking in Pictures*. New York: Doubleday, 1995.

Gray, C. (ed.). *The Morning News*. Newsletter available by subscription through Jenison Public Schools, Jenison, MI. (To order, call 616-457-8955.)

Gray, C. *The New Social Story Book*. Arlington, TX: Future Horizons, 1994.

Harrington, K. *For Parents and Professionals: Autism*. E. Moline, IL: LinguiSystems, Inc., 1998.

Hodgdon, L.A. *Visual Strategies for Improving Communication. Volume 1: Practical Supports for School and Home*. Troy, MI: Quirk Roberts Publishing, 1995.

Koski, P.S. *Autism & PDD: Picture Stories and Language Activities*. E. Moline, IL: LinguiSystems, Inc., 1998.

Mayer-Johnson, R. *Boardmaker* Software. Solana Beach, CA: Mayer-Johnson, 1995.

Richard, G.J. *The Source for Autism*. E. Moline, IL: LinguiSystems, Inc., 1997.

Rollins, P., Wambacq, I., Dowell, D., Mathews, L., and Reese, P. "An Intervention Technique for Children with Autistic Spectrum Disorder: Joint Attention Routines." *Journal of Communication Disorders*, Vol. 31, 1998, pp. 181-193.

19-09-17